Endless SUMMER

54 Quick and Creative Ice Cream and Dessert Recipes

With Sauces & Toppings

TRISH LOBENFELD

Library of Congress Cataloging–in–Publication
data is available.

Published by Zoku, LLC
720 Monroe Street, Suite C308
Hoboken, NJ 07030
www.zokuhome.com

ISBN: 978-0-988-31582-2

First Printing 2014

10 9 8 7 6 5 4 3 2 1

Printed in China

ART DIRECTOR
Melissa Secco

BOOK DESIGNER
Theresa Lennahan

ADDITIONAL DESIGN AND PRODUCTION
Sandie Burke

PHOTOGRAPHY AND RETOUCHING
Melissa Goodwin

PROP STYLISTS
Jason May
Will Nickley

MANAGING DIRECTOR
Ken Zorovich

ADDITIONAL COPYWRITING
Terin Izil

A very special thank you to tasters Frank, Karen and Julia; Hannah and her dad, Dennis; Scarlett Machson and Lynn Machson; Andy Payne and Rosie Perillo; Deb and Alex Rose; Paivi, Alexa, Juliana, Francesca and Christopher Simpson; and Sean Michael Street. Robyn B. Crain, thank you for recipe testing.

*We dedicate this book to the endless days
of summer, the memories they create,
and the people we've shared them with.*

Contents

Introduction

INGREDIENTS

Freshness is key to excellent ice cream. Check the dates on dairy and egg products to be sure you're using the freshest. Fruit should be plump, free of soft spots or discoloration. Local and seasonal fruit is always preferred — it has the best flavor and since it doesn't travel far, can be picked at peak ripeness and brought directly to market. A little Kosher salt is added to most recipes to enhance flavor and is preferred because it lacks the iodine taste in regular table salt.

DAIRY

Milk and cream are the main components in making ice cream and full fat products are used in these recipes. If possible, purchase pasteurized cream instead of ultra pasteurized. The higher heat treatment of ultra-pasteurized heavy cream destroys some of the qualities that provide a thick, rich texture and it sometimes has an off flavor. Yes, you can substitute low-fat or non-fat milk (in uncooked bases only), but this changes the texture of the ice cream to an icier, firmer consistency. Frozen yogurts are made with non-fat Greek yogurt, which has a delightful tang and a thicker texture than regular yogurt. Sour cream and soft cheeses such as, mascarpone, ricotta, and cream cheese are substituted for some portion of milk and/or cream in a few recipes for different texture and flavor.

NON-DAIRY

We've included a non-dairy section of frozen desserts using soy milk and almond milk, which create an icy, less creamy dessert. Coconut milk, on the other hand, has a high fat content and makes a softer textured frozen dessert; it separates during refrigeration, so be sure to stir well before using.

SWEETENERS

Granulated sugar plays an important role in making frozen desserts besides adding sweetness. It absorbs water and lowers freezing temperature, which keeps ice crystals smaller for a smooth, creamy texture. Other sweeteners, such as brown sugar, maple syrup and light agave syrup are used either in combination with granulated sugar or singly. Light corn syrup provides shine in chocolate sauces.

EGGS

French custards made with egg yolks, sugar, milk and sometimes cream have a smoother, creamier texture than Philly style ice cream, which uses dairy only. The yolk contains protein and lecithin. Protein coagulates when heated and creates an internal web that traps water and prevents large ice crystal formations. Lecithin, a natural emulsifier, binds fat and water together, and this, too, improves creaminess and texture. Some of the gelato recipes also use egg yolks for these reasons.

FLAVORINGS (INCLUDING ALCOHOL)

There are many ingredients that can be added to ice cream to add flavor. Because freezing lowers the sensory qualities of food, we've made bold use of extracts, teas, coffee, spices, cocoa powder and chilies. The addition of small pieces of chopped nuts, chocolate, and fresh or dried fruit adds texture and more flavor. Cut into small pieces, about 1/4 inch. Alcohol is a great way to enhance flavor. However, it slows the freezing process because it requires a lower freezing point, and should always be added at the end of the freezing process.

STORAGE

The finished ice cream has a similar consistency to soft-serve ice cream and freezing for an hour or two firms it for better scooping. Freeze in an airtight container to prevent the ice cream from absorbing any odors. Place a sheet of plastic wrap over the top if there's lots of headroom between the cover and the ice cream to prevent crystallization and freezer burn. Quickly return leftovers to the freezer to maintain the best quality.

FOOD SAFETY

Dairy products and eggs are highly perishable and subject to bacterial contamination with time and temperature abuse. Always keep items in the refrigerator until needed and replace immediately. Even though egg mixtures are cooked slightly, the eggs are not pasteurized. Use a cold-water bath to chill a cooked ice cream base and then refrigerate for proper cooling.

TIPS & TRICKS

Look for "Tips and Tricks" throughout the book for helpful suggestions on cooking techniques and additional clarification for a successful outcome.

RECIPE DIFFICULTY

Identify the difficulty of each recipe by the number of scoops on the ice cream cone. One scoop, very easy. Double-scoop cone, some cooking involved, moderately difficult. Triple-scoop cone, more complex, some cooking experience useful.

Equipment

APPLIANCES

Electric mixer (either handheld or upright): to make cookie dough and whip eggs.

Countertop blender or food processor: to puree solids into a liquid for the ice cream base, such as fresh fruit or cream cheese.

Zoku Ice Cream Maker or ice cream machine: to freeze the ice cream.

TOOLS

Baking tray and pan
Cutting board
Citrus juicer (hand or electric)
Knives (chef knife and paring knife)
Measuring utensils
Mixing bowls
Saucepan
Spatula
Strainer
Thermometers
Whisk
Wooden spoon
Vegetable peeler
Zester

STORAGE & SERVING

Quart-size covered containers
Ice cream scoop

easy   moderate   complex

TIPS and TRICKS

The Zoku Ice Cream Maker works best with fresh, chilled ingredients. Using room temperature ingredients, or using more than 5 ounces of recipe mixture may result in longer freezing times.

ZOKU
Ice Cream Maker

MAKE ICE CREAM FAST!

The Zoku Ice Cream Maker is fun for ice cream chefs of any age. Nobody likes to wait for ice cream and neither do we, so we created a way to watch it freeze in minutes. You'll be inventing your own flavors in no time, but here are a few recipes to break the ice. Just follow these simple steps: chill the mixture, pour 5 oz into the Zoku Ice Cream Maker, and Watch It Freeze! Within minutes your spoon will be working overtime.

We've got recipes from Philly-Style classics like Chocolate and Vanilla to avant-garde French Style to delizioso gelato and many, many more. Plus all your favorite ice cream–supporting roles like fresh apple pie, caramel sauce, and crunchy toppings. So many recipes, you can keep cool in any season. Or invent your own flavor by adding your favorite treats to your favorite frozen sweet.

Each ice cream recipe makes 1 quart of mix, enough to fill 6 Zoku Ice Cream Makers and make 6 happy ice cream eaters. All recipes are designed to be used with other ice cream makers as well. Just follow the instruction manual included with your ice cream maker for churning and freezing directions.

DIRECTIONS

Use chilled ingredients to make the ice cream mixtures, re-chill if necessary before pouring into the frozen bowl. Ideal temperature is 40°F/4.4°C or less.

Freeze the Zoku Ice Cream Maker bowl for 12+ hours (0°F/-18°C) before using.

STEP 1
Freeze inner bowl overnight for 12+ hours before using. Make sure inner bowl is completely dry before placing it in the freezer.

STEP 2
Pour 5 oz of chilled (40°F/4.4°C) ice cream mixture from fridge into frozen bowl from the freezer.

STEP 3
Stir, scrape, & add toppings; begin scraping bowl with provided spoon immediately. Stir and scrape frequently removing ice cream from the sides of the bowl.

WATCH IT FREEZE!

Philly Style

When you "all scream for ice cream" chances are you're screaming for Philadelphia-style. This crowd-pleaser is also known as "fresh ice cream" because there's no cooking involved—just churning milk, cream, sugar, and any flavor addition you can imagine. It pairs perfectly with any dessert in any season. Philly Style is great for beginner ice cream artisans of all ages. Just mix in your favorite additions and enjoy!

Neapolitan

America's most popular ice cream flavor is vanilla and chocolate is a close runner up. Another classic flavor is strawberry. Take a scoop each of strawberry, chocolate and vanilla and create your very own Neapolitan ice cream dessert.

Vanilla

1 ½ cups whole milk

1 ½ cups heavy cream

⅔ cup granulated sugar

1 tablespoon, plus 1 teaspoon vanilla extract

¼ teaspoon Kosher salt

DIRECTIONS

Whisk together the milk, cream, sugar, vanilla extract and salt in a medium-size bowl for three minutes, or until the sugar is dissolved. Chill ice cream mixture and stir well before using.

FREEZE

Follow the instructions included with your ice cream maker for churning and freezing.

MAKES 1 QUART *or* 6 ZOKU SERVINGS

Chocolate

1 ½ cups heavy cream

¾ cup granulated sugar

¼ cup Dutch-processed cocoa powder, sifted

4 ounces bittersweet chocolate, shaved

¼ teaspoon Kosher salt

1 ½ cups whole milk

1 tablespoon vanilla extract

DIRECTIONS

Bring the cream, sugar, cocoa powder, chocolate and salt to a boil in a medium-size saucepan, stirring constantly until cocoa powder is dissolved and chocolate is melted. Transfer to a bowl or storage container and stir in the milk and vanilla extract. Chill ice cream mixture and stir well before using.

FREEZE

Follow the instructions included with your ice cream maker for churning and freezing.

MAKES 1 QUART *or* 6 ZOKU SERVINGS

Strawberry

1 ½ cups rinsed and hulled fresh strawberries

½ cup granulated sugar

2 tablespoons freshly squeezed lime juice

1 teaspoon vanilla extract

¼ teaspoon Kosher salt

1 ¼ cups heavy cream

1 ¼ cups whole milk

DIRECTIONS

Puree the strawberries, sugar, lime juice, vanilla extract and salt in a blender or food processor. Add the cream and milk and pulse to combine. Chill ice cream mixture and stir well before using.

FREEZE

Follow the instructions included with your ice cream maker for churning and freezing.

MAKES 1 QUART *or* 6 ZOKU SERVINGS

TIPS *and* TRICKS

To maximize the strawberry flavor, cut large strawberries in quarters and small ones in half to get a full measure.

Almond
CHOCOLATE OATMEAL
Crunch

Who says oatmeal is only for breakfast? This recipe is cool blend of almond ice cream and homemade chocolate oatmeal raisin cookies. Don't worry, there will be plenty of extra cookies left over because this recipe was written by one smart cookie!

Chocolate Oatmeal Raisin Cookies

1 ½ cups all-purpose flour

⅔ cup cocoa powder

2 teaspoons baking powder

½ teaspoon Kosher salt

1 cup (2 sticks) unsalted butter

1 cup light brown sugar

½ cup granulated sugar

2 large eggs

1 tablespoon almond extract

1 teaspoon vanilla extract

1 cup quick-cooking oatmeal

½ cup bittersweet chocolate chips/chunks

½ cup raisins

½ cup whole almonds, coarsely chopped

DIRECTIONS

Preheat the oven to 350°F/177°C and lightly grease a cookie sheet.

Sift together the flour, cocoa powder, baking powder and salt into a small bowl and set aside.

Beat the butter and sugars in a mixing bowl fitted with the paddle attachment; scrape the sides and beater as needed. Once the butter is fluffy, add the eggs and almond and vanilla extracts. Beat, scraping as needed, until incorporated.

Add one-half of the flour mixture to the mixing bowl and mix on low until the flour is moist. Scrape the sides and beater and add the remaining flour mixture. Beat, scraping as needed, until the cookie dough is smooth. Stir in the oatmeal, chocolate, raisins and almonds.

Drop generous spoonfuls onto the onto the cookie sheet about two-inches apart and bake in the preheated oven for 15 minutes. Remove to a cooling rack and let sit a couple minutes on the sheet before using a spatula to slide onto the cooling rack. Cool completely; store in an airtight container.

MAKES 3 DOZEN COOKIES

Almond Ice Cream

1 ½ cups whole milk

1 ½ cups heavy cream

⅔ cup granulated sugar

1 tablespoon almond extract

¼ teaspoon Kosher salt

4 cookies cut into ½-inch pieces

DIRECTIONS

Whisk together the milk, cream, sugar, almond extract and salt in a medium-size bowl; cover and chill ice cream mixture. Stir well before using. Gently fold in the cookie pieces after the churning process.

FREEZE

Follow the instructions included with your ice cream maker for churning and freezing.

MAKES 1 QUART *or* 6 ZOKU SERVINGS

Peanut BUTTER

½ cup creamy natural peanut butter with salt

¾ cup granulated sugar

1 teaspoon vanilla extract

2 cups whole milk

1 cup heavy cream

DIRECTIONS

Whisk together the peanut butter, sugar and vanilla extract. Add the milk and cream in small increments at first, whisking with each addition, until the peanut butter loosens up. Whisk in the remaining liquid and cover. Chill ice cream mixture and stir well before using.

FREEZE

Follow the instructions included with your ice cream maker for churning and freezing.

MAKES 1 QUART *or* 6 ZOKU SERVINGS

TIPS *and* TRICKS

Top a scoop of peanut butter ice cream with a little strawberry sauce (page 74) for a delicious PB&J sundae! Like it crunchy? Swap crunchy peanut butter for creamy.

Mint CHOCOLATE CHIP

1 ½ cups whole milk

1 ½ cups heavy cream

⅔ cup granulated sugar

1 tablespoon mint extract

¼ teaspoon Kosher salt

4 ounces bittersweet chocolate, chopped into ¼-inch pieces

DIRECTIONS
Whisk together the milk, cream, sugar, mint extract and salt in a medium-size bowl. Chill ice cream mixture and stir well before using.

ADDITIONS
Add the chocolate three-quarters of the way through the freezing process.

FREEZE
Follow the instructions included with your ice cream maker for churning and freezing.

MAKES 1 QUART *or* 6 ZOKU SERVINGS

Maple WALNUT

Sweet and creamy with a nutty crunch; use real maple syrup for the best flavor.

1 ½ cups whole milk

1 ½ cups heavy cream

⅓ cup pure maple syrup

½ cup granulated sugar

1 tablespoon maple extract

¼ teaspoon Kosher salt

½ cup walnuts, chopped into ¼-inch pieces

DIRECTIONS
Whisk together the milk, cream, maple syrup, sugar, maple extract and salt in a medium-size bowl. Chill ice cream mixture and stir well before using.

ADDITIONS
Add the nuts three-quarters of the way through the freezing process.

FREEZE
Follow the instructions included with your ice cream maker for churning and freezing.

MAKES 1 QUART *or* 6 ZOKU SERVINGS

Espresso

We love the aroma of freshly brewed coffee and the jolt it gives you to start the day. Need a pick-me-up for the afternoon? Have a scoop of Espresso Ice Cream!

¼ cup hot water

2 tablespoons instant coffee

1 teaspoon instant espresso

¼ teaspoon Kosher salt

1 ½ cups whole milk

1 ½ cups heavy cream

¾ cup granulated sugar

2 teaspoons vanilla extract

DIRECTIONS
Whisk the hot water, instant coffee, instant espresso and salt in a medium-size bowl until dissolved. Stir in the milk, cream, sugar and vanilla extract. Chill ice cream mixture and stir well before using.

FREEZE
Follow the instructions included with your ice cream maker for churning and freezing.

MAKES 1 QUART *or* 6 ZOKU SERVINGS

Caramel Sauce

1 ½ cups granulated sugar

½ cup cold water

½ teaspoon sea salt

¼ teaspoon lemon juice

1 cup warm heavy cream

DIRECTIONS

Combine the sugar, water, sea salt and lemon juice in a medium-size saucepan; bring to a boil, stirring occasionally, until the sugar is dissolved. Reduce the heat to low and continue cooking until the sugar turns golden amber. If browning occurs in spots, carefully swirl the pan to disperse; don't use a spoon.

Remove the pan from the heat and slowly pour the warm cream in increments whisking constantly. If the sugar hardens (cream is too cold), return to the heat and cook until dissolved. Pour the sauce into a storage container and cool. Cover and refrigerate. To use: warm in the microwave on low or heat slowly in a saucepan.

CAUTION

Cooking with sugar is tricky business and requires patience. Have plenty of time and focus solely on the caramel to prevent the sugar from crystallizing or overcooking the sauce, which results in burnt, bitter caramel. The sugar reaches 350°F/177°C and sampling will burn your mouth. Warming the cream before using keeps the caramel from hardening, but it still comes to an immediate boil when it hits the caramel, be watchful of spitting and spattering.

MAKES 2 CUPS

Caramel & Sea Salt

1 ¼ cups chilled caramel sauce

1 ½ cups heavy cream

1 ¼ cups whole milk

Garnish: sea salt (optional)

DIRECTIONS

Whisk the caramel sauce and a little cream in a medium-size bowl to loosen the caramel, add more cream in small amounts until completely liquid. Stir in the remaining cream and milk. Chill ice cream mixture and stir well before using.

ADDITIONS

Garnish with a pinch of sea salt.

FREEZE

Follow the instructions included with your ice cream maker for churning and freezing.

MAKES 1 QUART *or* 6 ZOKU SERVINGS

Caramel
AND SEA SALT

Caramel and sea salt are all the rage and for good reason. The briny salt nicely complements the bitterness of the caramel. Garnish your ice cream with small pinches of sea salt, adding a little more sea salt as you work your way to the bottom of the bowl.

TIPS and TRICKS

When making caramel use a larger pan. Ingredients will overflow when milk/cream hits the sugar. Also, pour slowly! The cream boils immediately due to the high heat of the sugar.

French Cream

For the crème de la crème of ice cream, look no farther than France because nobody knows desserts better. And it's no surprise they have their own style of ice cream. It's rich. It's chic. It's magnifique! Whatever your ice cream du jour, you'll taste the time and care that goes into each step of this unique process. What gives it that je ne sais quois? Cooking then cooling a creamy custard. One lick and you'll feel like you're strolling along the Champs-Élysées. Perfect your technique with French Vanilla, then build your own Eiffel Tower of delicious scoops and say merci for beaucoup flavors.

French Vanilla

TIPS and TRICKS

Dress the waffle wafers, cones and bowls up by dipping the rims in melted chocolate, let set a minute and sprinkle with chopped nuts or colorful sprinkles.

French Vanilla

6 egg yolks

¾ cup granulated sugar

2 cups whole milk

1 cup heavy cream

1 vanilla bean, split and seeds scraped out

¼ teaspoon Kosher salt

DIRECTIONS

Set up a cold-water bath: a large bowl with a 50/50 mix of cold water and ice. Place a smaller bowl in the center with a mesh strainer over the bowl.

Beat the egg yolks and sugar until thoroughly combined, set aside.

Heat the milk, cream, vanilla bean (seeds and pod) and salt in a medium-size saucepan over medium heat until the milk begins to bubble around the edges of the pan. Pour the hot milk slowly into the egg and sugar, whisking constantly. Return the custard to the saucepan and cook over medium heat, stirring constantly, until thickened. The custard is done when you run your finger down the back of a coated spoon and it leaves a line, about 170°F/77°C. Don't let the custard come to a boil or the eggs scramble.

Strain the custard into the clean bowl and chill for 30 minutes, stirring occasionally. Stir well before using.

FREEZE

Follow the instructions included with your ice cream maker for churning and freezing.

MAKES 1 QUART or 6 ZOKU SERVINGS

Chocolate Waffle Wafers, Cones & Bowls

2 large eggs

½ cup granulated sugar

¼ teaspoon Kosher salt

4 tablespoons unsalted butter, melted

1 teaspoon vanilla extract

⅓ cup all-purpose flour

3 tablespoons Dutch-process cocoa powder

DIRECTIONS

Beat the eggs, sugar and salt in an electric mixer, fitted with the whisk attachment, or whisk by hand until the eggs lighten in color. Stir in the melted butter and vanilla extract. Fold in the flour and cocoa powder until moist, then beat until the batter is smooth.

Follow the instructions included with your waffle maker.

SHAPES

Cone: Use the cone mold that came with your waffle maker machine to wrap the wafer around, hold for a few seconds, let cool.

Ice cream dish: place a ½-cup ramekin upside down on a flat surface and center the wafer over the bottom, use a towel to press the sides down tight around the ramekin and hold a few seconds. Let cool.

Waffle wafers: use a 3-inch diameter cookie cutter to cut rounds, squares or any other shape for waffle wafers.

MAKES 8 WAFERS

Chocolate
MOCHA LATTE

Chocolate and coffee are soulmates; each enhances the flavor and aroma of the other. Combine them with a creamy egg custard and you have a luscious take on a frozen chocolate mocha latte.

6 egg yolks

¾ cup granulated sugar

2 cups whole milk

1 cup heavy cream

4 ounces dark or bittersweet chocolate, cut into small pieces

1 tablespoon instant espresso

¼ teaspoon Kosher salt

DIRECTIONS

Set up a cold-water bath: a large bowl with a 50/50 mix of cold water and ice. Place a smaller bowl in the center with a mesh strainer over the bowl.

Beat the egg yolks and sugar until thoroughly combined, set aside.

Heat the milk, cream, chocolate, espresso and salt in a medium-size saucepan over medium heat until the milk begins to bubble around the edges of the pan; if the chocolate isn't melted by then, stir off heat.

Pour the hot milk slowly into the egg and sugar, whisking constantly. Return the custard to the saucepan and cook over medium heat, stirring constantly, until thickened. The custard is done when you run your finger down the back of a coated spoon and it leaves a line, about 170°F/77°C. Don't let the custard come to a boil or the eggs scramble.

Strain the custard into the clean bowl and chill for 30 minutes, stirring occasionally. Cover and refrigerate at least five hours or overnight. Stir well before using.

FREEZE

Follow the instructions included with your ice cream maker for churning and freezing.

MAKES 1 QUART *or* 6 ZOKU SERVINGS

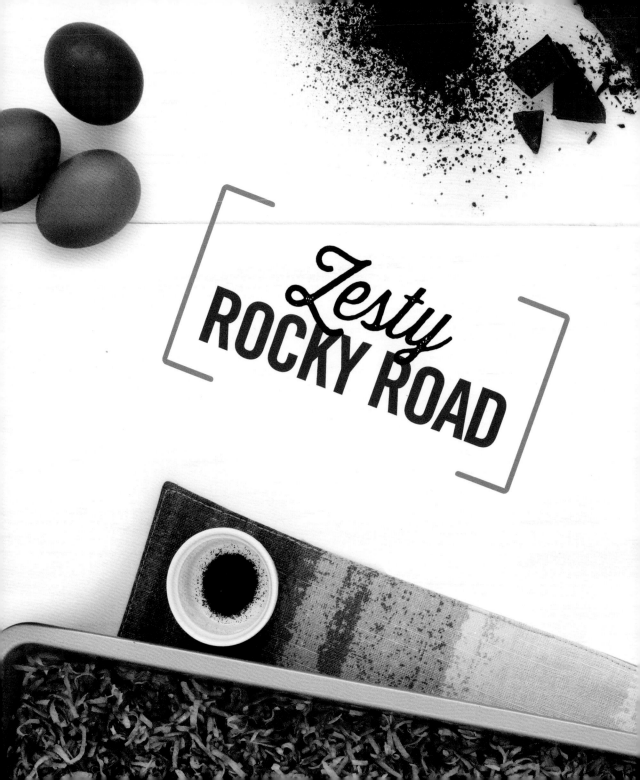

Zesty
ROCKY ROAD

For an extra special twist, add ¼ cup toasted pepitas, either with the almonds or in lieu of the almonds.

4 large egg yolks

⅔ cup granulated sugar

1 ½ cups whole milk

¾ cup heavy cream

4 ounce bittersweet chocolate bar, cut into tiny pieces

¼ cup Dutch-processed cocoa, sifted

¼ teaspoon Kosher salt

1 tablespoon orange zest

2 teaspoons orange extract*

⅓ cup sweetened coconut flakes

½ cup mini marshmallows

¼ cup toasted slivered almonds, slightly chopped

2 tablespoons orange liqueur, such as Cointreau or Grand Marnier (optional)

DIRECTIONS

Set up a cold-water bath: a large bowl with a 50/50 mix of cold water and ice. Place a smaller bowl in the center with a mesh strainer.

Beat the egg yolks and sugar until thoroughly combined, set aside.

Heat the milk, cream, chocolate, cocoa powder and salt in a medium-size saucepan over medium heat until the milk begins to bubble around the edges of the pan; if the chocolate and cocoa are not dissolved, stir off heat until melted. Pour the hot milk slowly into the egg and sugar, whisking constantly. Return the custard to the saucepan and cook over medium heat, stirring constantly, until thickened. The custard is done when you run your finger down the back of a coated spoon and it leaves a line, about 170°F/77°C. Don't let the custard come to a boil or the eggs scramble.

Strain the custard into the clean bowl and chill for 30 minutes, stirring occasionally. Stir in the orange extract, if using, cover and chill ice cream mixture. Stir well before using.

ADDITIONS

*If you plan to add the orange liqueur, skip the orange extract.

Add the coconut, marshmallows, nuts and orange liqueur, if desired, three-quarters of the way through the freezing process.

FREEZE

Follow the instructions included with your ice cream maker for churning and freezing.

MAKES 1 QUART _or_ 6 ZOKU SERVINGS

Limoncello
BASIL

Limoncello Basil

4 egg yolks

¾ cup granulated sugar

1 ½ cups whole milk

1 ½ cups heavy cream

1 large basil sprig

¼ teaspoon Kosher salt

¼ cup freshly squeezed lemon juice

1 ½ teaspoons lemon zest

1 teaspoon lemon extract

1 tablespoon finely chopped basil

2 tablespoons lemon Vodka (optional)

DIRECTIONS

Set up a cold-water bath: a large bowl with a 50/50 mix of cold water and ice. Place a smaller bowl in the center with a mesh strainer over the bowl.

Beat the egg yolks and sugar until thoroughly combined, set aside.

Heat the milk, cream, basil and salt in a medium-size saucepan over medium heat until the milk begins to bubble around the edges of the pan. Pour the hot milk slowly into the egg and sugar, whisking constantly. Return the custard to the saucepan and cook over medium heat, stirring constantly, until thickened. The custard is done when you run your finger down the back of a coated spoon and it leaves a line, about 170°F/77°C. Don't let the custard come to a boil or the eggs scramble.

Strain the custard into the clean bowl and chill for 30 minutes, stirring occasionally. Stir in the lemon juice, lemon zest and lemon extract, cover and refrigerate ice cream mixture. Stir well before using.

ADDITIONS

Add the lemon vodka three-quarters of the way through the freezing process. Fold in the basil last.

FREEZE

Follow the instructions included with your ice cream maker for churning and freezing.

MAKES 1 QUART or 6 ZOKU SERVINGS

Carrot Cake with FROSTING

This recipe has it all, the cream cheese "frosting," carrots for texture and aromatic spices. Dig in!

---

6 egg yolks

¾ cup granulated sugar

2 cups whole milk

1 eight-ounce package cream cheese, cut into 12 cubes

½ cup chopped peeled carrots

½ teaspoon ground cinnamon

¼ teaspoon ground allspice

⅛ teaspoon ground nutmeg

¼ teaspoon Kosher salt

1 teaspoon vanilla extract

½ cup chopped walnuts (optional)

DIRECTIONS

Set up a cold-water bath: a large bowl with a 50/50 mix of cold water and ice. Place a smaller bowl in the center.

Beat the egg yolks and sugar until thoroughly combined, set aside.

Heat the milk, cream cheese, carrots, cinnamon, allspice, nutmeg and salt in a medium-size saucepan over medium heat until the milk begins to bubble around the edges of the pan. Pour the hot milk slowly into the egg and sugar, whisking constantly. Return the custard to the saucepan and cook over medium heat, stirring constantly, until thickened. The custard is done when you run your finger down the back of a coated spoon and it leaves a line, about 170°F/77°C. Don't let the custard come to a boil or the eggs scramble.

Pour the custard into the clean bowl and chill for 30 minutes, stirring occasionally. Stir in the vanilla extract, cover and chill ice cream mixture. Stir well before using.

ADDITIONS

Add the chopped walnuts three-quarters of the way through the freezing process.

FREEZE

Follow the instructions included with your ice cream maker for churning and freezing.

MAKES 1 QUART *or* 6 ZOKU SERVINGS

TIPS *and* TRICKS

The carrot cake custard is not strained; the carrot pieces are essential to the flavor and texture; an experienced hand is best here.

Rum RAISIN

½ cup raisins

½ cup dark rum

5 egg yolks

¾ cup granulated sugar

1 ½ cups whole milk

1 ½ cups heavy cream

¼ teaspoon Kosher salt

1 tablespoon rum extract

DIRECTIONS

Combine the raisins and rum in a small microwaveable bowl or a small saucepan. Warm for 30–40 seconds in the microwave or for one minute on the stovetop over low heat. Let the raisins macerate overnight.

Set up a cold-water bath: a large bowl with a 50/50 mix of cold water and ice. Place a smaller bowl in the center with a mesh strainer over the bowl.

Beat the egg yolks and sugar until thoroughly combined, set aside.

Heat the milk, cream and salt in a medium-size saucepan over medium heat until the milk begins to bubble around the edges of the pan. Pour the hot milk slowly into the egg and sugar, whisking constantly. Return the custard to the saucepan and cook over medium heat, stirring frequently, until thickened. The custard is done when you run your finger down the back of a coated spoon and it leaves a line, about 170°F/77°C. Don't let the custard come to a boil or the eggs scramble.

Strain the custard into the clean bowl and chill for 30 minutes, stirring occasionally. Add the rum extract, cover and chill ice cream mixture. Stir well before using. Use a slotted spoon to scoop the raisins into the Ice Cream Maker about three-quarters of the way through the freezing process. Discard any remaining rum.

FREEZE

Follow the instructions included with your ice cream maker for churning and freezing.

MAKES 1 QUART *or* 6 ZOKU SERVINGS

TIPS and TRICKS

The key to success with this recipe is to macerate the raisins in the rum overnight. They plump up and absorb almost all the rum and stay soft in the ice cream. Intoxicating!

White Chocolate
WITH FUDGE SWIRL

Your mouth will be swirling with delight with white chocolate and chocolate fudge in every bite.
This twist on tradition is a feast for the eyes, just be careful not to get hypnotized!

---

4 egg yolks

²⁄₃ cup granulated sugar

1 ½ cups whole milk

1 cup heavy cream

4 ounces white chocolate chips
or small chunks

¼ teaspoon Kosher salt

¾ cup hot fudge sauce
(see recipe on page 76)

DIRECTIONS

Set up a cold-water bath: a large bowl with a 50/50 mix
of cold water and ice. Place a smaller bowl in the center
with a mesh strainer over the bowl.

Beat the egg yolks and sugar until thoroughly combined,
set aside.

Heat the milk, cream, chocolate and salt in a medium-size
saucepan over medium heat until the milk begins to
bubble around the edges of the pan; if the chocolate isn't
melted by then, stir off heat. Pour the hot milk slowly into
the egg and sugar, whisking constantly. Return the custard
to the saucepan and cook over medium heat, stirring
constantly, until thickened. The custard is done when you
run your finger down the back of a coated spoon and it
leaves a line, about 170°F/77°C. Don't let the custard come
to a boil or the eggs scramble.

Strain the custard into the clean bowl and chill for 30
minutes, stirring occasionally. Stir well before using.

Once the ice cream is frozen, use the Zoku Ice Cream
Maker spoon to make a small hole in the ice cream and
drop in a generous teaspoonful of chilled hot fudge
sauce. Cover using the Zoku spoon and repeat six or
seven more times at different spots and depths. Place in
the freezer for 10-20 minutes.

FREEZE

Follow the instructions included with your ice cream maker
for churning and freezing.

MAKES 1 QUART *or* 6 ZOKU SERVINGS

TIPS *and* TRICKS

Work carefully when spreading the ice cream over the fudge. If you smudge the sauce, it streaks the ice cream and the ice cream looks muddy when scooped.

Pumpkin PIE

4 egg yolks

¾ cup granulated sugar

1 ½ cups whole milk

1 cup heavy cream

¾ teaspoon ground cinnamon

¼ teaspoon ground ginger powder

¼ teaspoon ground allspice

¼ teaspoon Kosher salt

1 cup raw, plain pumpkin

1 teaspoon vanilla extract

DIRECTIONS

Set up a cold-water bath: a large bowl with a 50/50 mix of cold water and ice. Place a smaller bowl in the center with a mesh strainer over the bowl.

Beat the egg yolks and sugar until thoroughly combined, set aside.

Heat the milk, cream, cinnamon, ginger, allspice and salt in a medium-size saucepan over medium heat until the milk begins to bubble around the edges of the pan Pour the hot milk slowly into the egg and sugar, whisking constantly. Return the custard to the saucepan and cook over medium heat, stirring constantly, until thickened. The custard is done when you run your finger down the back of a coated spoon and it leaves a line, about 170°F/77°C. Don't let the custard come to a boil or the eggs scramble.

Strain the custard through the strainer into the clean bowl and chill for 30 minutes, stirring occasionally. Stir in the pumpkin and the vanilla extract, cover and chill ice cream mixture. Stir well before using.

FREEZE

Follow the instructions included with your ice cream maker for churning and freezing.

MAKES 1 QUART *or* 6 ZOKU SERVINGS

TIPS *and* TRICKS

Purchase raw, plain pumpkin, not raw
pumpkin pie mix with the spices included.

Nutella

6 egg yolks

½ cup granulated sugar

1 ½ cups whole milk

1 cup Nutella

½ cup heavy cream

¼ teaspoon Kosher salt

1 teaspoon vanilla extract

½ cup toasted hazelnuts (optional)

DIRECTIONS

Preheat the oven to 350°F/177°C.

Spread the hazelnuts across a baking sheet and pop into the preheated oven for ten minutes. Remove the hazelnuts and slide them onto a dishtowel, wrap and set aside for ten minutes. Rub the hazelnuts inside the towel to remove the skins (some skins will remain and that's okay). Transfer to a cutting board and chop into very small pieces.

Set up a cold-water bath: a large bowl with a 50/50 mix of cold water and ice. Place a smaller bowl in the center with a mesh strainer over the bowl.

Beat the egg yolks and sugar until thoroughly combined, set aside.

Heat the milk, Nutella, cream and salt in a medium-size saucepan over medium heat until the milk begins to bubble around the edges of the pan and the Nutella is dissolved. Pour the hot milk slowly into the egg and sugar, whisking constantly. Return the custard to the saucepan and cook over medium heat, stirring constantly, until thickened. The custard is done when you run your finger down the back of a coated spoon and it leaves a line, about 170°F/77°C. Don't let the custard come to a boil or the eggs scramble.

Strain the custard into the clean bowl and chill for 30 minutes, stirring occasionally. Stir in the vanilla extract, cover and chill ice cream mixture. Stir well before using.

ADDITIONS

Add the toasted hazelnuts three-quarters of the way through the freezing process.

FREEZE

Follow the instructions included with your ice cream maker for churning and freezing.

MAKES 1 QUART *or* 6 ZOKU SERVINGS

Desserts

There are no better words to see on a dessert menu than a la mode. So why not do the same at home? Add a scoop of fresh ice cream to your favorite pie. Sandwich it between two different kinds of perfectly baked cookies. Complement the rich taste of a chocolately brownie. Cold, creamy ice cream pairs perfectly with any dessert, making any sweet even sweeter. So let your imagination play chef and make your sweet tooth sing.

Apple Pie A LA MODE

Double-Crust

2 ½ cups all-purpose flour

1 cup (2 sticks) unsalted butter, cut into 16 pieces

1 tablespoon granulated sugar

1 teaspoon Kosher salt

¾ cup cold water

DIRECTIONS

Pulse the flour, butter, sugar and salt in the base of a food processor fitted with the mixing paddle attachment until the butter is the size of peas. Add ¼-cup water and pulse to combine.

Add the flour to a large bowl and add another ¼-cup cold water and gently toss the flour with your fingers. Grab a small handful and press together; if the dough crumbles, add more water by the tablespoon, toss and check again. Repeat as needed until the dough holds it shape. Form two round balls of dough and place each on a square of plastic wrap, cover and press down with the flat of your hand to form a disk. Refrigerate for at least 30 minutes.

Preheat the oven to 350°F/177°C and butter a 10-inch deep-dish pie pan.

In the meantime, prepare your pie filling.

MAKES 8 PIE SLICES

TIPS and TRICKS

For a more interesting and complex pie, use at least three types of apples, such as Granny Smith, McIntosh and Rome. Dried fruit and nuts provide texture and the fruit plumps with the apple juices.

Apple Pie Filling

9 apples, peeled, cored and cut into ¼-inch slices

2 tablespoons freshly squeezed lemon juice

¼ cup granulated sugar

2 tablespoons all-purpose flour

1 teaspoon ground cinnamon

¼ cup coarsely chopped walnuts (optional)

¼ cup dried fruit, such as raisins or cranberries (optional)

1 tablespoon unsalted butter, cut into 6 pieces

1 large egg, beaten

DIRECTIONS

Toss together the apples and lemon juice to coat well. Sprinkle half the sugar, flour and cinnamon over the apples and toss. Sprinkle the remaining sugar, flour and cinnamon over the apples and toss again.

Prepare a lightly floured surface and roll out the first pastry disk to a 13-inch round. Place it in the bottom of the pan, pressing the sides down to create a flat bottom.

Sprinkle the remaining tablespoon of flour on the bottom of the pie crust. Add ⅓ of the pie filling to the pie pan, moving the apples to fit snuggly. Sprinkle ⅓ of the nuts and dried fruit, if using, over the apple. Add another ⅓ pie filling and sprinkle ⅓ of the nuts and dried fruit. Repeat with the remaining pie filling, nuts and dried fruit. Make sure everything is packed well and dot the top of the pie with six pieces of the butter.

Roll out the second disc and drape over the filled pie. Trim the edges of the crust with a paring knife leaving a 1-inch border. Roll the edge under all the way around the pie and then crimp the crust. Brush the top and edges generously with the egg wash and slit a few steam holes in the top of the pie with the paring knife.

Place on a pie drip pan and bake in the preheated oven for 1½ hours. Test the apples by slipping a knife through the top vent hole; the apples should offer no resistance and the crust should be golden brown, if not, continue baking until apples are soft. Remove and cool. Pour juices from the drip pan back into the pie through the top steam vent or around the rim of the crimped crust.

PERFECT PAIR

This recipe pairs perfectly with Caramel & Sea Salt Ice Cream on page 22. For a more traditional pair, serve with Vanilla Ice Cream on page 14.

Mini Cookie
SANDWICHES

¾ cup unsalted butter

1 cup light brown sugar

½ cup granulated sugar

2 large eggs

1 large egg yolk

1 tablespoon vanilla extract

1 teaspoon Kosher salt

2 cups all-purpose flour

1 ½ teaspoons baking soda

1 ½ cups chocolate chips

½ cup chopped nuts (optional)

DIRECTIONS
Preheat the oven to 350°F/177°C. Lightly grease a cookie sheet or 11-inch by 15-inch by 1-inch baking pan.

Beat the butter and sugars in an electric mixer fitted with the paddle attachment; scrape the sides and beater as needed. Once the butter is fluffy, add the eggs, egg yolk, vanilla extract and salt. Beat, scraping sides and beater as needed until incorporated.

Add one cup flour and the baking soda to the bowl and mix on low until the flour is moist. Scrape the sides and beater and add the final cup of flour. Beat, scraping as needed, until the cookie dough is smooth.

ADDITIONS
Stir in the chocolate chips and nuts, if using, such as, walnuts, pecans or slivered almonds.

Cookies: Drop by the spoonful onto the cookie sheet 1 ½-inches apart. Bake in the preheated oven for 14 minutes or until lightly brown. Remove to a cooling rack and let sit a couple of minutes on the sheet before using a spatula to slide onto the cooling rack. Cool completely; store in an airtight container.

Sheet tray: Spread the cookie dough in the baking pan and bake in preheated oven for 15 minutes, or until center is set. Remove and cool. Use a cookie cutter to make different shape ice cream sandwich cookies.

Scoop ¼ cup ice cream onto the bottom of one cookie, top with another cookie and press gently to spread the ice cream to the edges; use an offset spatula or table knife to smooth the sides. Roll the sides in sprinkles or mini chocolate chips as an added touch.

MAKES ~ 3 ½ DOZEN COOKIES

PERFECT PAIR
Pictured with Vanilla and Chocolate Ice Cream on pages 14 & 15. This recipe also pairs perfectly with half Peanut Butter and half Chocolate on pages 18 & 15.

Cheesecake RED VELVET Brownie Bar

½ cup unsalted butter, cut into 8 pieces

2 ounces unsweetened chocolate, cut into small pieces

1 cup granulated sugar

2 large eggs

1 teaspoon vanilla extract

¾ cup all-purpose flour

½ cup chopped walnuts

DIRECTIONS

Preheat the oven to 350°F/177°C and lightly grease a 9-inch x 9-inch pan.

Melt the butter and chocolate slowly in a double boiler or in a microwave-safe bowl in the microwave stirring occasionally. Remove from the heat and stir in the sugar; blend well. Add the eggs and vanilla extract and beat lightly, without incorporating much air. Fold in the flour until all the flour has been incorporated then stir in the walnuts.

Spread the mixture into the greased baking pan and put into the preheated oven. Bake 20–25 minutes. The brownies are done when a toothpick inserted in the middle shows a moist crumb.

Transfer to a cooling rack. Once cool, wrap tightly and freeze.

New York Style Cheesecake Ice Cream

12 ounces cream cheese

¾ cup granulated sugar

2 teaspoons vanilla extract

¼ teaspoon Kosher salt

1 ½ cups whole milk

DIRECTIONS

Puree the cream cheese, sugar, vanilla extract, salt and one-half cup milk in a blender or food processor. Add more milk and pulse to loosen the mixture. Add remaining milk and pulse to combine. Chill ice cream mixture and stir well before using.

FREEZE

Follow the instructions included with your ice cream maker for churning and freezing.

MAKES 1 QUART *or* 6 ZOKU SERVINGS

Red Velvet Ice Cream

2 cups heavy cream

⅔ cup granulated sugar

¼ cup Dutch-processed cocoa powder, sifted

¼ teaspoon Kosher salt

1 ½ cups buttermilk

1 teaspoon red food dye

1 teaspoon vanilla extract

DIRECTIONS

Bring the cream, sugar, cocoa powder and salt to a boil in a medium-size saucepan over medium heat. Stir continuously to dissolve the cocoa powder. Transfer to a storage container and stir in the buttermilk, red dye and vanilla extract. Chill ice cream mixture and stir well before using.

FREEZE

Follow the instructions included with your ice cream maker for churning and freezing.

MAKES 1 QUART *or* 6 ZOKU SERVINGS

Brownie Bar Assembly

Remove the brownie bar from the freezer and spread freshly made or slightly softened cheesecake ice cream over the brownie. Return to the freezer for 30 minutes. Remove and spread the freshly made or slightly softened red velvet ice cream across the cheesecake ice cream. Return to the freezer for at least two hours

To serve dip a chef's knife in hot water and cut into 16 bars, rinsing the knife in hot water as needed.

MAKES 16 BARS

Profiteroles
WITH RASPBERRY SAUCE

1 cup cold water

½ cup unsalted butter, cut into 8 pieces

½ teaspoon Kosher salt

1 cup all-purpose flour

4 large eggs

glaze: 1 egg and a pinch of salt, beaten

DIRECTIONS

Preheat the oven to 425°F/218°C and line a baking tray with parchment paper.

Bring the water, butter and salt to a boil in a medium-size saucepan. Add the flour off heat and stir with a wooden spoon until thoroughly blended into a smooth paste. Return to the heat to cook the flour for another four minutes, stirring constantly, to gelatinize the starch and evaporate some of the water.

Transfer the dough into a mixing bowl fitted with a paddle attachment and beat at medium speed to cool, about one minute. Add the first egg and beat until completely absorbed, scraping the bowl and beater as needed. Continue one egg at a time.

Scoop the dough in a pastry bag fitted with a 1-inch straight tip and pipe 2-inch rounds on the lined baking tray. Moisten the tip of your finger with cold water and gently flatten any peaks on top to prevent burning. Brush the shells with the egg glaze and bake in the preheated oven for 12 minutes, lower the heat to 350°F/177°C and continue cooking for 20 minutes. Turn the oven off and let the profiteroles sit for 10 minutes before removing. The shells should be golden brown outside and dry and hollow inside. Cool completely and store in an airtight container. Reheat at 350°F/177°C for 5 minutes to crisp.

Slice off the top and set aside. Fill each bottom with a scoop of ice cream. Replace the tops and spoon sauce over the top. Serve immediately.

PERFECT PAIR

Pictured with Vanilla Ice Cream and Raspberry Sauce pages 14 & 74. This recipe also pairs perfectly with Zesty Rocky Road Ice Cream and Marshmallow Sauce on pages 30 & 74.

MAKES 10-12 SHELLS

Gelato

When you taste a spoonful of rich, creamy gelato, it's hard not to imagine you're sitting on the Spanish Steps looking out at Rome. That's because gelato has been tied to Italian culture for thousands of years. Based on the Italian word for frozen, gelato is made with fresh fruits and nuts and contains very little air, giving it a smooth, silky consistency. Don't forget to toss a coin in the Trevi Fountain to wish for more gelato before returning back to reality. So whip up some gelato and ciao down!

Hoboken CANNOLI

*Hoboken is the birthplace of Zoku, Frank Sinatra and baseball. The film classic **On the Waterfront**, starring Marlon Brando, was filmed in Hoboken. With a strong Italian heritage associated with the city it seemed only right to name a gelato after our famous hometown.*

---

1 cup mascarpone cheese

1 cup ricotta cheese

¾ cup powdered sugar

1 cup whole milk

½ cup heavy cream

1 teaspoon lemon zest (1 medium lemon)

½ teaspoon vanilla extract

¼ teaspoon ground cinnamon

¼ teaspoon Kosher salt

¼ cup finely chopped pistachio nuts

DIRECTIONS

Whisk together the cheeses, sugar, milk, cream, lemon zest, vanilla extract, cinnamon and salt in a medium-size bowl. Chill gelato mixture and stir well before using.

ADDITIONS

Add the finely chopped pistachios about three-quarters of the way through the freezing process.

FREEZE

Follow the instructions included with your ice cream maker for churning and freezing.

MAKES 1 QUART *or* 6 ZOKU SERVINGS

Tiramisu

1 cup mascarpone cheese

1 ½ cups whole milk

⅔ cup granulated sugar

¼ cup heavy cream

1 teaspoon vanilla extract

¼ teaspoon Kosher salt

¼ cup chocolate covered espresso beans, gently crushed with the side of a knife

6 Lady Fingers, cut into ¼-inch slices lengthwise

1 tablespoon coffee liqueur, such as Illy or Kahlua

garnish: cocoa powder or shaved dark chocolate curls (optional)

DIRECTIONS

Whisk the mascarpone cheese, milk, sugar, cream, vanilla extract and salt in a medium-size bowl until smooth and sugar is dissolved, about three minutes. Chill gelato mixture and stir well before using.

While the gelato is churning, drizzle the liqueur over the chopped Lady Fingers and toss to combine. Fold in the Lady Fingers and the chocolate covered espresso beans.

ADDITIONS

Garnish and serve with a light dusting of cocoa powder or a few shaved chocolate curls.

FREEZE

Follow the instructions included with your ice cream maker for churning and freezing. Remove the mixing paddle (if using a standard ice cream maker) before folding in the Lady Fingers and the chocolate covered espresso beans.

MAKES 1 QUART *or* 6 ZOKU SERVINGS

Eggnog WITH BOURBON

Don't wait until the holiday season for eggnog. This is a rich, creamy frozen version lightly perfumed with cinnamon and nutmeg.

6 egg yolks

¾ cup granulated sugar

2 cups heavy cream

1 cup whole milk

½ teaspoon ground cinnamon

¼ teaspoon ground nutmeg

¼ teaspoon Kosher salt

2 tablespoons bourbon extract

2 tablespoons bourbon whiskey (optional)

garnish: freshly grated nutmeg (optional)

DIRECTIONS

Set up a cold-water bath: a large bowl with a 50/50 mix of cold water and ice. Place a smaller bowl in the center with a mesh strainer over the bowl.

Beat the egg yolks and sugar until thoroughly combined, set aside.

Heat the cream, milk, cinnamon, nutmeg and salt in a medium-size saucepan over medium heat until the milk begins to bubble around the edges of the pan. Pour the hot milk slowly into the egg and sugar, whisking constantly. Return the custard to the saucepan and cook over medium heat, stirring constantly, until thickened. The custard is done when you run your finger down the back of a coated spoon and it leaves a line, about 170°F/77°C. Don't let the custard come to a boil or the eggs scramble.

Strain the custard through the strainer into the clean bowl and chill for 30 minutes, stirring occasionally. Stir in the bourbon extract, and chill gelato mixture. Stir well before using.

ADDITIONS

Add the bourbon whiskey about three-quarters of the way through the freezing process. Garnish each serving with freshly grated nutmeg.

FREEZE

Follow the instructions included with your ice cream maker for churning and freezing.

MAKES 1 QUART *or* 6 ZOKU SERVINGS

DE LECHE

Dulce de Leche is long-cooked sweetened condensed milk, which caramelizes and thickens into a sauce. Use the left over cold sauce to create a swirl that makes it doubly delicious.

Dulce de Leche Sauce

2 cans (15 ounces each) sweetened condensed milk

DIRECTIONS

Preheat the oven to 450°F/232°C.

Pour the condensed milk into a shallow baking dish and cover tightly with foil. Set this dish inside a roasting pan and fill with hot water until it rises halfway up the side of the baking dish. Bake for two hours; don't let the pan go dry, refill with hot water as needed. Remove from the oven, transfer to a storage container and whisk until smooth and cool. Refrigerate.

Dulce de Leche

¾ cups cold Dulce de Leche sauce

1 ½ cups whole milk

1 cup heavy cream

1 teaspoon vanilla extract

¼ teaspoon Kosher salt

¾ cup cold Dulce de Leche

DIRECTIONS

Whisk a little milk into the Dulce de Leche in a medium-size bowl to loosen it up. Add the remaining milk, cream, vanilla extract and salt and whisk vigorously to combine. Chill ice cream mixture and stir well before using.

Once the ice cream is frozen, use the Zoku spoon to make a small hole in the ice cream and drop in a generous teaspoonful of cold Dulce de Leche. Cover using the Zoku spoon and repeat six or seven more times at different spots and depths. Place in the freezer for 10-20 minutes.

FREEZE

Follow the instructions included with your ice cream maker for churning and freezing.

MAKES 1 QUART *or* 6 ZOKU SERVINGS

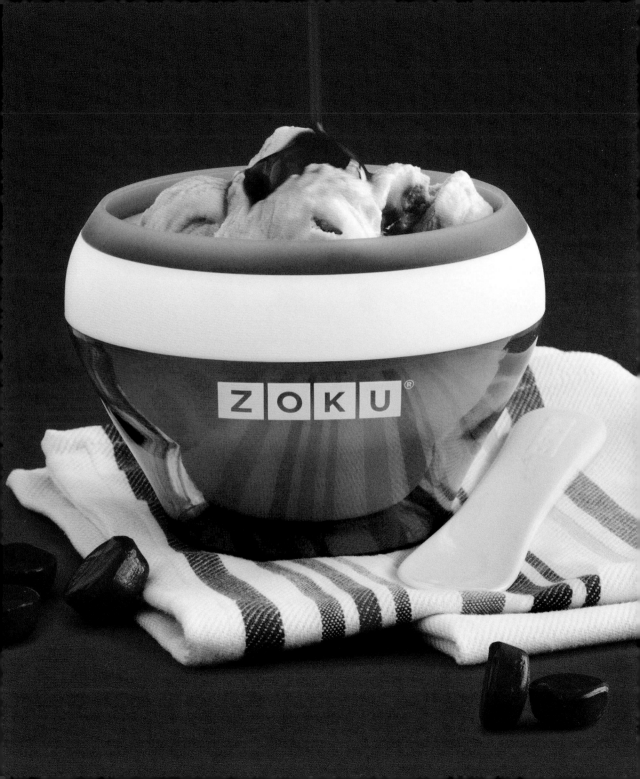

Ricotta
CHEESECAKE

Ricotta Cheesecake

6 egg yolks

¾ cup granulated sugar

1 cup whole milk

¾ cup heavy cream

¼ teaspoon Kosher salt

1 ½ cups whole milk ricotta cheese

1 tablespoon orange zest
(1 medium orange)

1 teaspoon lemon zest
(1 medium lemon)

1 1/2 teaspoons vanilla extract

DIRECTIONS

Set up a cold-water bath: a large bowl with a 50/50 mix of cold water and ice. Place a smaller bowl in the center with a mesh strainer over the bowl.

Beat the egg yolks and sugar until thoroughly combined, set aside.

Heat the milk, cream and salt in a medium-size saucepan over medium heat until the milk begins to bubble around the edges of the pan. Pour the hot milk slowly into the egg and sugar, whisking constantly. Return the custard to the saucepan and cook over medium heat, stirring frequently, until thickened. The custard is done when you run your finger down the back of a coated spoon and it leaves a line, about 17°F/77°C. Don't let the custard come to a boil or the eggs scramble.

Strain the custard into the clean bowl and stir in the ricotta cheese, orange and lemon zests. Chill for 30 minutes, stirring occasionally. Stir in the vanilla extract, cover and chill ice cream mixture. Stir well before using.

FREEZE

Follow the instructions included with your ice cream maker for churning and freezing.

MAKES 1 QUART *or* 6 ZOKU SERVINGS

Summer Raspberry

2 cups fresh raspberries

1/4 cup water

1/4 teaspoon Kosher salt

5 large egg yolks

3/4 cup granulated sugar

1 1/4 cups whole milk

1 cup heavy cream

DIRECTIONS

Combine the raspberries, water and salt in a small saucepan and bring to a boil. Cook down the raspberries until they no longer hold their shape, stirring occasionally, about ten minutes. Strain the raspberries into a clean medium-size bowl using the back of a soup spoon or small rubber spatula to scrape the pulp through the mesh. Discard the seeds.

Set up a cold-water bath: a large bowl with a 50/50 mix of cold water and ice. Place a smaller bowl in the center with a mesh strainer over the bowl.

Beat the egg yolks and sugar until thoroughly combined, set aside.

Heat the milk and cream in a medium-size saucepan over medium heat until the milk begins to bubble around the edges of the pan. Pour the hot milk slowly into the egg and sugar, whisking constantly. Return the custard to the saucepan and cook over medium heat, stirring frequently, until thickened. The custard is done when you run your finger down the back of a coated spoon and it leaves a line, about 170°F/77°C. Don't let the custard come to a boil or the eggs scramble.

Strain the custard through the strainer into the clean bowl, stir in the raspberry puree and chill for 30 minutes, stirring occasionally. Stir well before using.

FREEZE

Follow the instructions included with your ice cream maker for churning and freezing.

MAKES 1 QUART *or* 6 ZOKU SERVINGS

Frozen Yogurt

Whether you call it fro-yo, frogurt, or just plain frozen yogurt, we can all agree that enjoying a bowl of this distinctively tart treat is one of the best ways to chill out. As its name would imply, this ice-cold style is made by freezing Greek yogurt. It's the perfect blank canvas for creativity. So mix in your favorite flavors and get ready to yell Opa!

Graham Cracker
S'MORE

S'more Frozen Yogurt

1 ½ cups marshmallow sauce (page 74)

1 ½ cups nonfat Greek yogurt

1 teaspoon vanilla extract

¼ teaspoon Kosher salt

½ cup mini marshmallows

¼ cup chopped milk chocolate, chopped into ¼-inch pieces

¼ cup chopped graham crackers, chopped into ¼-inch pieces

DIRECTIONS

Whisk the marshmallow sauce, yogurt, vanilla extract and salt together in a medium-size bowl. Chill frozen yogurt mixture and stir well before using. Fold in the marshmallows, chocolate and cracker pieces or chocolate-covered graham cracker pieces.

FREEZE

Follow the instructions included with your ice cream maker for churning and freezing. Remove the mixing paddle (if using a standard ice cream maker) and fold in the marshmallows, chocolate and cracker pieces or chocolate-covered graham cracker pieces.

MAKES 1 QUART or 6 ZOKU SERVINGS

Frozen Yogurt Sandwich

Scoop ¼ cup frozen yogurt onto the bottom of one graham cracker half and top with another half. Press gently to spread the frozen yogurt. Use an offset spatula or table knife to smooth the edges. Dip edges in mini chocolate chips or sprinkles for an added touch.

Chocolate-Covered Graham Crackers (optional)

8 ounces milk chocolate cut into small pieces

6–8 graham crackers, cut in half widthwise

DIRECTIONS

Stovetop method: Fill the bottom of a double boiler ⅓ full of water and bring to a boil. Lower the heat and cover with the top of the double boiler. Melt the chocolate in the top pan, stirring gently until completely melted.

Microwave method: Melt the chocolate in a medium-size microwave safe bowl on low temperature, stopping two or three times to stir. Reheat the chocolate as needed during the dipping process.

Dip each cracker individually into the melted chocolate covering completely. Hold the cracker over the bowl and let the excess chocolate drip off; lay on a sheet of wax paper to set.

Banana
CHOCOLATE

Banana Chocolate Frozen Yogurt

1 cup packed sliced banana (about 2 small bananas)

$^2/_3$ cup granulated sugar

$^1/_2$ cup cocoa powder

1 tablespoon banana extract

$^1/_4$ teaspoon Kosher salt

2 $^1/_2$ cups nonfat Greek yogurt

$^1/_2$ cup peanut butter chips, chopped small (optional)

DIRECTIONS
Puree the bananas, sugar, cocoa powder, banana extract, salt and one cup of the yogurt in a blender or food processor. Add the remaining yogurt and pulse to combine. Chill frozen yogurt mixture and stir well before using.

ADDITIONS
Add the peanut butter chips, if using, three-quarters of the way through the freezing process.

FREEZE
Follow the instructions included with your ice cream maker for churning and freezing.

MAKES 1 QUART *or* 6 ZOKU SERVINGS

Honey Frozen Yogurt

$^1/_2$ cup honey

1 teaspoon vanilla extract

$^1/_4$ teaspoon Kosher salt

3 $^1/_2$ cups nonfat Greek yogurt

DIRECTIONS
Combine the honey, vanilla extract and salt in a medium-size bowl. Whisk 1/4-cup yogurt into the honey to loosen. Gradually whisk in the remaining yogurt. Chill frozen yogurt mixture and stir well before using.

FREEZE
Follow the instructions included with your ice cream maker for churning and freezing.

MAKES 1 QUART *or* 6 ZOKU SERVINGS

TIPS *and* TRICKS
Try a robust flavored honey such as buckwheat, maple, or sumac to complete the tangy frozen yogurt.

Sauces
AND TOPPINGS

These ice cream recipes are so scrumptious, they're hard to top. Unless you use these hard-to-resist sauces and toppings. Forget the cherry—drizzle on fresh Pineapple, Strawberry, or Raspberry Sauce instead. Or make your own Marshmallow Sauce, so good you'll want s'more. Heat things up with freshly made Hot Fudge. Whichever you choose, these additions are ready to drizzle, drip, and drop on your favorite ice cream.

Marshmallow Sauce

2 large egg whites

1/4 teaspoon cream of tartar

1/4 teaspoon Kosher salt

3/4 cup cold water

1/3 cup granulated sugar

1/3 cup light corn syrup

1/4 cup whole milk

1 teaspoon vanilla extract

DIRECTIONS

Beat the egg whites on low in an electric mixer fitted with the whisk attachment until foamy. Add the cream of tartar and salt and continue beating on medium-high to the "stiff peak" stage.

Combine the water, sugar and corn syrup in a small saucepan and bring to a boil. Continue cooking until the "soft ball" stage, 240°F/116°C, using a candy thermometer or laser thermometer to gauge the temperature.

Turn the mixer on medium speed and slowly pour the syrup down the side of the bowl and beat until the eggs become thick and shiny. Beat until the mixture cools slightly, scrape sides and beater, add the milk and vanilla extract and beat for another minute. Store in a covered container in the refrigerator.

MAKES 2 CUPS

Raspberry Sauce

3 cups fresh raspberries, rinsed

1/4 cup granulated sugar

1/4 cup cold water

1/4 teaspoon salt

2 tablespoons raspberry-flavor liqueur, such as Chambord (optional)

DIRECTIONS

Combine the raspberries, sugar, water and salt in a small saucepan over medium heat. Cook down the raspberries until they no longer hold their shape, stirring occasionally, about ten minutes. Strain the raspberries into a clean bowl using the back of a soup spoon or rubber spatula to scrape the pulp through the mesh. Discard the seeds. Stir in the raspberry-flavor liqueur, if using. Cover, cool, and refrigerate.

MAKES 2 CUPS

Strawberry Sauce

3 cups fresh strawberries, rinsed and hulled

$\frac{1}{2}$ cup cold water

$\frac{1}{4}$ cup granulated sugar

$\frac{1}{4}$ teaspoon salt

2 tablespoons strawberry liqueur,
such as Fragoli (optional)

DIRECTIONS

Combine the strawberries, water, sugar and salt in a small saucepan over medium heat. Cook down the strawberries until they no longer hold their shape, stirring occasionally, about ten minutes. Puree in a blender or food processor with the liqueur, if using. Transfer to a storage container, cool, and refrigerate.

MAKES 2 CUPS

Pineapple Sauce

2 cups diced fresh pineapple

$\frac{1}{4}$ cup cold water

$\frac{1}{4}$ cup granulated sugar

$\frac{1}{4}$ teaspoon salt

DIRECTIONS

Bring the pineapple, water, sugar and salt to a boil in a small saucepan. Lower the heat a bit and continue cooking, stirring occasionally, until the pineapple no longer holds its shape, about 15 minutes. Puree in a blender or food processor. Transfer to a storage container, cool slightly and refrigerate.

MAKES 2 CUPS

And more!

CARAMEL SAUCE
See Caramel and
Sea Salt recipe, page 22

DULCE DE LECHE SAUCE
See Dulce de Leche
recipe, page 62

TIPS *and* TRICKS

For chocolate-covered mini pretzels and Quick Shells, make a double boiler using a small saucepan and a metal bowl that fits tightly over the top.

Chocolate-Covered Mini Pretzels

8 ounces chocolate (dark, milk, or white), cut into small pieces

3 heaping cups mini pretzels

DIRECTIONS

Stovetop method: Fill the bottom of a double boiler $\frac{1}{3}$ full of water and bring to a boil. Lower the heat and cover with the top of the double boiler. Melt the chocolate in the top pan, stirring gently until completely melted.

Microwave method: Melt the chocolate in a medium-size microwave safe bowl on low temperature, stopping two or three times to stir. Reheat the chocolate as needed during the dipping process.

Fully-covered pretzels: Add the pretzels to the melted chocolate one cup at a time, stir to coat completely and remove with tweezers or a fork letting excess chocolate drip back into the pan, then lie flat on wax paper to set.

Partially-covered pretzels: Dip each pretzel individually into the melted chocolate to the desired depth, let the excess chocolate drip back into the pan, then lie flat on wax paper to set.

MAKES A GENEROUS 3 CUPS

Hot Fudge Sauce

1 cup heavy cream

$\frac{3}{4}$ cup Dutch-process cocoa powder, sifted

$\frac{2}{3}$ cup dark brown sugar

$\frac{1}{3}$ cup light corn syrup

4 tablespoons unsalted butter, cut into four pieces

1 teaspoon instant coffee

$\frac{1}{4}$ teaspoon Kosher salt

1 teaspoon vanilla extract

DIRECTIONS

Combine the cream, cocoa powder, sugar, corn syrup, butter, instant coffee and salt in a small sauce pan and bring to a boil; lower the heat a bit and continue cooking and stirring until the sugar and cocoa powder are dissolved. Transfer to a storage container and cool. Stir in vanilla extract, cover and refrigerate. To use, warm slowly in the microwave or a saucepan over low heat.

MAKES 2 CUPS

Chocolate Sauce

1 cup whole milk

4 ounces bittersweet chocolate, cut into small pieces

$\frac{1}{2}$ cup granulated sugar

$\frac{1}{2}$ cup light brown sugar

2 tablespoons Dutch-process cocoa powder, sifted

$\frac{1}{4}$ teaspoon salt

1 teaspoon vanilla extract

DIRECTIONS

Bring the milk, chocolate, sugars, cocoa powder and salt to a boil in a medium-size saucepan. Lower the heat a bit and cook, stirring constantly, until melted and smooth. Transfer to a storage container, cool, stir in vanilla extract and refrigerate.

MAKES 2 CUPS

Quick Shell

$\frac{2}{3}$ cup (4 oz) semi-sweet chocolate chips

$\frac{1}{3}$ cup (2 1/2 oz) refined coconut oil

DIRECTIONS

In a double boiler over barely simmering water, whisk together the chocolate chips and coconut oil until the chocolate has completely melted. Remove from heat and let cool completely before applying to ice cream.

WHITE CHOCOLATE VARIATION

Substitute the semi-sweet chips with white chocolate chips.

MAKES ¾ CUP

And more!

CHOCOLATE-COVERED GRAHAM CRACKERS

See Graham Cracker S'mores recipe, page 68.

Dairy Free

Change up the milk in your ice cream to add even more flavor to your next bowl. Coconut milk adds a tropical twist to flavors like Thai Coconut Ginger Jalapeño. Almond milk sweetens the deal in Middle Eastern Basmati Rice. And soy milk steals the show in a spoonful of Banana Soy. With even more dairy-free possibilities floating around in your mind, you'll want to milk it for all it's worth. In fact, these dairy free ice creams are so tasty, you'll want to be enjoying them long after the cows come home.

BASMATI RICE

Basmati Rice Pudding Custard

4 egg yolks

³⁄₄ cup granulated sugar

1 ½ cups almond milk

½ teaspoon ground cinnamon

¼ teaspoon Kosher salt

pinch ground nutmeg

2 teaspoons vanilla extract

1 cup well-cooked Basmati rice

DIRECTIONS

Set up a cold-water bath: a large bowl with a 50/50 mix of cold water and ice. Place a smaller bowl in the center with a mesh strainer over the bowl.

Beat the egg yolks and sugar until thoroughly combined and set aside.

Heat the almond milk, cinnamon, salt and nutmeg in a medium-size saucepan over medium heat until the milk begins to bubble around the edges of the pan. Pour the hot milk slowly into the egg and sugar, whisking constantly. Return the custard to the saucepan and cook over medium heat, stirring constantly, until thickened. The custard is done when you run your finger down the back of a coated spoon and it leaves a line, about 170°F/77°C. Don't let the custard come to a boil or the eggs scramble.

Strain the custard into the clean bowl and chill for 30 minutes, stirring occasionally. Stir in the vanilla extract.

While the custard is cooling, prepare the rice.

Rice

4 cups cold water

¹⁄₃ cup Basmati rice

2 teaspoons Kosher salt

2 teaspoons vanilla extract

DIRECTIONS

Bring the water, rice and salt to a boil; lower the heat a bit and continue cooking for about 20 minutes or until the rice is very tender. Drain and put the rice in a blender. Add 1 cup almond custard and puree. Add the remaining almond custard and the vanilla extract and pulse to combine. Chill ice cream mixture and stir well before using.

FREEZE

Follow the instructions included with your ice cream maker for churning and freezing.

MAKES 1 QUART *or* 6 ZOKU SERVINGS

TIPS *and* TRICKS

The heat in chilies comes from the pith, the little vein inside, not the seeds; leave it attached for more heat, if desired.

---

1 can (15 ounces) coconut cream

1 can (13.5 ounces) coconut milk

$2/_3$ cup granulated sugar

4 bruised lemongrass stalks, cut into chunks

3 one-inch pieces peeled ginger, smashed

1 large jalapeño, split in half, seeds removed

$1/_4$ teaspoon Kosher salt

2 tablespoons freshly squeezed lime juice

$1/_4$ cup crystallized ginger, cut into $1/_4$-inch pieces

DIRECTIONS

Set up a cold-water bath: a large bowl with a 50/50 mix of cold water and ice. Place a smaller bowl in the center with a mesh strainer over the bowl.

Bring the coconut cream, coconut milk, sugar, lemongrass, ginger, jalapeño and salt to a boil in medium-sized sauce pan. Lower the heat and simmer for five minutes. Remove from the heat and steep for 20 minutes.

Strain the liquid into the bowl, discard the solids and chill for 30 minutes, stirring occasionally. Add the lime juice, cover and chill ice cream mixture. Stir well before using.

ADDITIONS

Add the crystallized ginger about three-quarters of the way through the freezing process.

FREEZE

Follow the instructions included with your ice cream maker for churning and freezing.

MAKES 1 QUART *or* 6 ZOKU SERVINGS

Banana SOY

This is a delicate dessert. The soy milk creates a fluffy textured dessert with the sweet flavor of ripe bananas. Kick it up a notch and add some chocolate chips and cover with strawberry sauce—so delicious!

1 cup packed sliced banana
(about 2 small bananas)

$^2/_3$ cup light agave nectar

2 teaspoons banana extract

$^1/_4$ teaspoon Kosher salt

1 $^1/_2$ cups plain soy milk

DIRECTIONS

Puree the banana, light agave nectar, banana extract, salt and $^1/_2$ cup soy milk in a blender or food processor. Chill ice cream mixture and stir well before using.

FREEZE

Follow the instructions included with your ice cream maker for churning and freezing.

MAKES 1 QUART *or* 6 ZOKU SERVINGS

Sorbet *and* GRANITA

It's easy for anyone to become a sorbet gourmet. Just grab your favorite fruits or juices and turn them into a frozen treat in minutes. Sorbets are brightly colored, richly flavored, and denser than many ice creams. They can be personalized with fresh fruit or toppings so you can serve sorbet your way.

When you've got a thirst to quench, granitas are your go-to dessert. These frozen concoctions are full of flavor and ice crystals, making it easy to crunch or gulp these fruity treats. Granitas are the perfect way to cool down on a hot summer day. In fact, they're so refreshing, they're often served with coffee or used as a palate cleanser. This traditional Sicilian dessert may be full of ice, but trust us, it's no clone of a snow cone.

Cranberry
POMEGRANATE LIME
Sorbet

2 cups fresh or frozen cranberries

¾ cups granulated sugar

¼ cup cold water

¼ teaspoon Kosher salt

1 ½ cups 100% pomegranate juice

1 tablespoon lime zest
(about 2 limes)

2 tablespoons freshly-squeezed lime juice

DIRECTIONS

Combine the cranberries, sugar, water and salt in a medium-size saucepan and bring to a boil; lower the heat a bit and continue cooking until the cranberries have softened, about ten minutes. Don't be alarmed when the berries make a popping noise as they burst.

Puree the cranberries in a blender or food processor. Add the pomegranate juice, lime zest and lime juice and pulse until combined. Chill sorbet mixture and stir well before using.

FREEZE

Follow the instructions included with your ice cream maker for churning.

MAKES 1 QUART *or* 6 ZOKU SERVINGS

White Russian Granita

3 ½ cups strong coffee

¾ cup granulated sugar

¼ teaspoon Kosher salt

1 teaspoon vanilla extract

2 tablespoons coffee liqueur, such as Illy or Kahlua

Garnish: 1 cup heavy cream, beaten until slightly thick (optional)

DIRECTIONS

Stir the coffee, sugar and salt together in a storage container until the sugar is dissolved, about three minutes. Cool slightly, stir in the vanilla extract, cover and chill granita mixture. Stir well before using.

ADDITIONS

Spoon a dollop of whipped cream over the top of each serving.

FREEZE

Follow the instructions included with your ice cream maker for churning.

If not using an ice cream maker, the following traditional technique may be used. Pre-chill a ceramic or glass container large enough to hold a little more than a quart in the freezer one-half hour before using. Pour in the chilled mix and freeze for 30 minutes. Remove and scrape the sides with a fork. Repeat this every 30 minutes for up to four hours, until the texture resembles Italian ice or a snow cone.

MAKES 1 QUART *or* 6 ZOKU SERVINGS

Mulled Apple Cider Granita

1 quart apple cider

²⁄₃ cup granulated sugar

2 tablespoons mulling spices (store bought) or use the mulling spices recipe below

DIRECTIONS

Set up a cold-water bath: a large bowl with a 50/50 mix of cold water and ice. Place a smaller bowl in the center with a mesh strainer over the bowl.

Bring the cider, sugar and mulling spices to a boil in a large saucepan. Lower the heat and simmer for 20 minutes. Strain the cider into the bowl and chill for 30 minutes, stirring occasionally. Chill granita mixture and stir well before using.

FREEZE

Follow the instructions included with your ice cream maker for churning.

If not using an ice cream maker, the following traditional technique may be used. Pre-chill a ceramic or glass container in the freezer one-half hour before using. Pour the chilled mix into the pre-chilled container and freeze for 30 minutes. Remove and scrape the sides with a fork. Repeat this every 30 minutes for three to four hours, until the texture resembles Italian ice or a snow cone.

MAKES 1 QUART *or* 6 ZOKU SERVINGS

Mulling Spices

1 tablespoon whole cloves

2 teaspoons crushed cassia

1 teaspoon allspice berries

1 whole nutmeg

3 whole cardamom pods

DIRECTIONS

Crush the nutmeg in a sealed plastic bag with a meat mallet or heavy-bottomed pan, measure ¼ teaspoon and save the rest. Gently crush the cardamom and use all.

Pink Grapefruit Thyme Sorbet

3 cups pink grapefruit juice and pulp
(about 3 large pink grapefruit)

⅓ cup granulated sugar

½ ripe avocado

2 tablespoons chopped fresh thyme leaves

DIRECTIONS
Puree the sugar and avocado with one-half cup grapefruit juice in a blender or food processor. Add the remaining juice and thyme and pulse to combine. Chill sorbet mixture and stir well before using.

FREEZE
Follow the instructions included with your ice cream maker for churning.

MAKES 1 QUART *or* 6 ZOKU SERVINGS

Blood Orange Granita

3 ¼ cups blood orange juice and pulp (10–12 oranges)

¾ cup granulated sugar

DIRECTIONS
Stir the orange juice/pulp and sugar together in a medium-size bowl until sugar is dissolved, about 3 minutes. Chill ice cream mixture and stir well before using.

FREEZE
Follow the instructions included with your ice cream maker for churning.

If not using an ice cream maker, the following traditional technique may be used. Pre-chill a ceramic or glass container in the freezer one-half hour before using. Pour the chilled mix into the pre-chilled container and freeze for 30 minutes. Remove and scrape the sides with a fork. Repeat this every 30 minutes for three to four hours, until the texture resembles an Italian ice or a snow cone.

MAKES 1 QUART *or* 6 ZOKU SERVINGS

Minty Melon Sorbet

3 ½ cups fresh cantaloupe chunks

1 cup mint simple syrup (recipe below)

2 tablespoons freshly squeezed lime juice

½ teaspoon Kosher salt

2 tablespoons thinly sliced fresh mint

DIRECTIONS
Puree the melon, simple syrup, lime juice and salt in a blender or food processor. Chill sorbet mixture and stir well before using. Fold in the mint before serving.

FREEZE
Follow the instructions included with your ice cream maker for churning.

MAKES 1 QUART *or* 6 ZOKU SERVINGS

Mint Simple Syrup

¾ cup granulated sugar

¾ cup cold water

10 large sprigs mint, ripped
and pinched to release essential oils

DIRECTIONS
Bring the sugar, water and mint to a boil in a small saucepan; lower the heat a bit and cook until the sugar is dissolved. Remove from the heat and steep for 20 minutes. Drain and discard the mint springs.

Index

Conversion CHARTS

Measurement Equivalent

AMOUNT		EQUALS	
1	tablespoon	3	teaspoons
1/16	cup	1	tablespoon
1/8	cup	2	tablespoons
1/6	cup	2	tablespoons + 2 teaspoons
1/4	cup	4	tablespoons
1/3	cup	5	tablespoons + 1 teaspoon
3/8	cup	6	tablespoons
1/2	cup	8	tablespoons
3/4	cup	12	tablespoons
1	cup	48	teaspoons or 16 tablespoons
8	fluid ounces (fl oz)	1	cup
1	pint	2	cups
1	quart	2	pints or 4 cups
1	gallon	4	quarts or 8 cups
16	ounces (oz)	1	pound (lb)

Volume

US		UK	
1/4	teaspoon	1.25	ml
1/2	teaspoon	2.5	ml
1	teaspoon	5	ml
1	tablespoon/ 3 teaspoons	15	ml
1	fl oz/2 tablespoons	30	ml
1/4	cup	60	ml
1/3	cup	80	ml
1/2	cup	120	ml
1	cup	240	ml
1	pint/2 cups	475	ml
1	quart/4 cups	950	ml
1	gallon/4 quarts	3.8	liters

Oven temperature

FAHRENHEIT	CELSIUS	UK GAS MARKS
200	95	-
250	120	1/2
275	135	1
300	150	2
325	165	3
350	175	4
375	190	5
400	200	6
450	230	8
500	260	10

Weight

US		UK	
1	oz	28	g
4	oz (1/4 lb)	113	g
8	oz (1/2 lb)	227	g
12	oz (3/4 lb)	340	g
16	oz (1 lb)	454	g